Contents

Introduction
What this book contains	3
How to set, mark and interpret the tests	3
Helping your child sit tests	4
What to do with the results	4
Testing your child's English	6
Setting the spelling test	7
Setting the comprehension test	8
Setting the reading test	9
Setting the writing test	11

Test 1
	12
Spelling picture 1	12
Spelling text 1	13
Comprehension test 1 – fiction	14
Comprehension test 1 – non-fiction	20
Reading test 1	24
Writing test 1	25

Test 2
	26
Spelling picture 2	26
Spelling text 2	27
Comprehension test 2 – fiction	28
Comprehension test 2 – non-fiction	34
Reading test 2	38
Writing test 2	39
Answers	40
Reading test assessment	46
Writing test assessment	47

Text © ST(P), Wendy Wren 1998

The right of ST(P), Wendy Wren to be identified as the author of this work has been asserted by her in accordance with the Copyright, Designs and Patents Act 1988.

The author and publishers wish to thank the following for permission to use copyright material: Mammoth for the excerpts from *Penguin's Progress* by Jill Tomlinson, Reed Consumer Books Limited, 1991; Macdonald & Co for excerpts from *William's Problems* by Shirley Isherwood, 1988; *1996 Key Stage 1 English Tasks: Reading and Writing Teacher's Handbook*, SCAA, 1995, Ref. KS1/95/322.

All rights reserved. No part of this publication may be reproduced or transmitted in any form or by any means, electronic or mechanical, including photocopy, recording or any information storage and retrieval system, without permission in writing from the publisher or under licence from the Copyright Licensing Agency Limited. Further details of such licences (for reprographic reproduction) may be obtained from the Copyright Licensing Agency Limited of 90 Tottenham Court Road, London W1P 9HE.

Designed by Ian Foulis & Associates, Saltash, Cornwall
Illustrated by Katerina Sardella and Mike Miller

This edition published exclusively for W H Smith, 1998, by
Stanley Thornes (Publishers) Ltd
Ellenborough House
Wellington Street
CHELTENHAM GL50 1YW

98 99 00 01 / 10 9 8 7 6 5 4 3 2 1

A catalogue record for this book is available from the British Library.

ISBN 0–7487–3579–8

Printed and bound in Spain by Mateu Cromo

Introduction

What this book contains

During your child's last year in infant school (Year 2) he or she will sit Key Stage 1 National Assessment Tests in the two core subjects: English and mathematics. These tests take place in school over a period of about a week during May and the results are reported back to you and are also passed on to the teacher of the Key Stage 2 class your child will attend. For each of the subjects your child will be given a mark in the form of a level. Most children will perform in the range of Levels 1–3 by the end of Key Stage 1 with an average performance being roughly Level 2.

The tests are a valuable measure of your child's performance in school. Not only will they be influential in the school's assessment of your child's progress, they may also be your child's first experience of sitting formal written tests. It is extremely helpful if that first experience can be a positive one.

This book provides you with two sets of English practice papers with the principal aim of preparing your child confidently for the tests. Each set of papers will:

- provide test questions similar to those in the National Tests for Levels 1–2a in English in the National Curriculum.

- give your child practice in sitting the tests: working to a set time, getting familiar with the format and style of the tests and developing effective test strategies.

- give you a broad guide to your child's likely level of performance within Levels 1–2a of the subject.

- give you an idea of strengths and weaknesses in your child's learning.

How to set, mark and interpret the tests

Each set of papers allows you to set, mark and level your child's work in English without any prior knowledge of the National Curriculum. First read the detailed advice on setting the papers; then set the test. When your child has finished each paper use the answers to mark it. Then use the conversion box at the end of the answers to get an idea of National Curriculum level.

INTRODUCTION

Helping your child sit tests

As well as practising the content of the tests, one of the key aims of this book is to give your child practice in working under test conditions. Although at Key Stage 1 tests are not timed, it is a good idea to allow your child a limited amount of time to complete the various tasks. The spelling test could take up to 30 minutes. In trials children working at Level 2 were able to complete the comprehension test (both fiction and non-fiction elements) within around 40 minutes. The length of time spent on the writing test will vary. Allow your child time to finish his or her piece of writing to his or her satisfaction. In order to make best use of the tests, and to ensure that the experience is a positive one for your child, it is helpful to follow a few basic principles:

- Talk with your child first before embarking on the tests. Present the activity positively and reassuringly. Encourage your child to view doing the papers as an enjoyable activity which will help, always making him or her feel secure about the process.

- Ensure that your child is relaxed and rested before doing a test. It may be better to do a paper at the weekend or during the holidays rather than straight after a day at school.

- Ensure a quiet place, free from noise or disturbance, for doing the tests.

- Ensure that there is a watch or clock available.

- Ensure that your child understands exactly what to do for each paper and give some basic test strategies for tackling the task. For example:

    - Try to tackle all the questions but don't worry if you can't do some. Put a pencil mark by any you can't do, leave them and come back at the end.
    - Make sure you read the questions carefully.
    - Go straight on to the next page when each is finished.
    - Try to pace yourself over the allowed time. Look over the whole paper first to get an idea of how many questions there are. Don't spend too long over one question.
    - Use all your time.
    - If you have any time over at the end go back over your answers. This is particularly important if you are doing one big piece of work, such as writing a story.

- Taking the time to talk over a test beforehand and to discuss any difficulties afterwards will really help your child to gain confidence in the business of sitting tests.

- However your child does, ensure that you give plenty of praise for effort.

What to do with the results

The tests in this book and the results gained from them are only a guide to your child's likely level of performance. They are not an absolute guarantee of how your child will actually perform in the National Tests themselves. However, these papers

INTRODUCTION

will at least allow your child to get practice in sitting tests; they will also give *you* an insight into the strengths and weaknesses in their learning.

If there are particular areas of performance which seem weaker, it may be worth providing more practice of the skills required. It is also valuable to discuss any such weaknesses with your child's class teacher, and to seek confirmation of any problem areas and advice on how to proceed. It is always better to work in partnership with the school if you can. Above all ensure that you discuss these issues with your child in a positive and supportive way so that you have their co-operation in working together to improve learning.

Testing your child's English

Introduction

Key Stage 1 tests are an important part of monitoring and assessing the progress and levels of attainment of 7-year-olds and, as such, should be seen as a diagnostic tool. Any kind of 'testing' can be intimidating, so letting children practise what they are expected to do serves two purposes.

1. It gives you more than just a 'snapshot' of your child's performance at one particular time.
2. It helps children become familiar with what is required, thus making them less likely to underachieve through nervousness in a new situation.

This book has two complete tests divided into the following sections:

- Spelling test – pictures and text

- Comprehension test – fiction and non-fiction

- Reading test – fiction

- Writing test

It is important to note that in the actual reading test, your child will be given a choice of books. It is impossible to recreate this, but to ensure that the reading passage is within a familiar context, it follows on from the comprehension tests, which your child should do first.

The different sections of the tests can be given individually to allow children to practise the areas in which they are weakest, or as a whole.

The introductory notes for each section summarise the design of the tests and the instructions you should give to your child. You can reword the instructions as you think fit. These notes are followed by the different sections of the tests and answers, marking and assessment criteria.

Setting the spelling test

1. This test is suitable for children whom you think are working within Level 2 or above in writing.

2. The tests are designed to enable children to show their ability when they are asked to concentrate solely on spelling.

3. The tests contain a range of words commonly known by 7-year-olds and have been taken mainly from the Group 1 list of *Essentials in Teaching and Testing Spelling* by Fred J Schonell, 1985.

4. Give your child a copy of the test and a pencil. Tell him/her to rub out or cross out answers they wish to change.

Picture spelling tests

1. Discuss the large picture with your child and the small pictures around it.

2. Make sure your child knows what each picture represents.

3. Ask your child to write the name of each small picture in the box underneath. You can remind him/her what the pictures are if he/she has forgotten.

Text spelling tests

1. The text test is thematically linked to the picture test so the children should feel comfortable with the context.

2. Ask your child to listen to you as you read out the complete text, which you will find on pages 40 and 43. You may find it helpful to make a copy of the passage to read out.

3. Ask your child to look at the text and note that some of the words are missing. These words are in bold type in the passages on pages 40 and 43.

4. Explain that when you read the text again your child should write in the missing words as you go along.

5. Reread the text, pausing to let the child write in wherever a word has been missed out. Each missing word may be repeated three times.

Setting the comprehension test

1   Each test is designed so that it can be completed in one session, but you may decide to have a break between the fiction and non-fiction passages.

2   There is no time limit for the test. Most children will probably be able to complete the test within 40 minutes.

3   Give your child a copy of the test and a pencil. Tell him/her to rub out or cross out answers they wish to change.

4   Do not help your child with the reading of the text. However, you may help with the spelling of the answers they wish to give. Do not penalise your child for spelling errors but encourage him/her to be as careful as possible.

5   Tell your child to read a page at a time and to try to answer the questions at the bottom of the page. Remind them that they:

- can rub out/cross out answers they wish to change,
- should tick only one box for each question,
- will find the answers on the same page as the question,
- should try every question.

6   Throughout the test you can remind your child of what he/she should be doing, i.e. read a page then answer the questions at the bottom of the page; turn over and read the next page, etc.

Setting the reading test

The test is designed to enable children to demonstrate their ability to:
- read aloud from a text;
- show what they have understood;
- give a personal response.

In the actual Key Stage 1 test, the child reads from a whole book. As it is impossible to recreate this exactly, the reading test here is a continuation of the comprehension passage, and as such should follow the comprehension test.

The reading test begins where the comprehension test finished. Each test has a marking grid and suggested questions.

1 Explain to your child that what he/she is going to read is part of the story which he/she has already done some work on in the comprehension test.

2 Reread the beginning of the story from the comprehension test. It is very important that the early part of the story, before the reading passage begins, is shared with your child, so that he/she can become familiar with the structure of the story and any names or specialised language used.

3 Ask your child to read aloud the passage and attempt any unfamiliar words.

4 Photocopy and use the grids on pages 42 and 45 to mark the following:
- O for any words omitted;
- T for any words you have to tell your child (words which the child needs in order to retain the sense of the passage);
- the exact word your child says when he/she makes an incorrect attempt.

5 Record the strategies your child uses to attempt to read unfamiliar words, whether they are T (told) or not, using the following codes:

Ph = phonic	knowledge of print symbols and sound patterns
G = graphic	knowledge of parts of words or consistent letter patterns, e.g. help for helping
S = syntactic	a grammatically sensible substitution, e.g. his/her, me/he
C = contextual	a sensible substitution within the meaning of the text as a whole, e.g. dirty for dusty
Sc = self correct	evidence of successful use of reading strategies

Discussing the book after reading

Following your child's reading you should discuss the whole text, i.e. the comprehension and reading passages, with your child.

Level 1

The discussion should focus on your child's ability to understand the text and identify aspects which he/she enjoyed or found interesting.

Questions which you might ask or adapt can be found following the marking grids for the passages, on pages 42 and 45.

What to look for
A range of appropriate responses to some of these questions will provide evidence of your child's understanding of and response to aspects of his/her reading.

Level 2

If your child is responding well, move on to explore his/her understanding of, and ability to express opinions about, the main events or ideas in the text. Begin by asking your child to tell you what has happened in the story so far and to talk about what might happen in the rest of the story.

Use the retelling to initiate a discussion during which your child is given the opportunity to respond to the story so far. Ask a range of questions with the aim of encouraging your child to talk about the meaning and significance of what he/she has read in order to gather evidence of his/her understanding of and response to the story.

Some examples of the sorts of question you might ask can be found following the marking grids, on pages 42 and 45.

What to look for
Responses to a range of questions of the type suggested will provide evidence of your child's understanding of and response to the story.

You should observe, for example, whether your child:
- has understood the main events or ideas in the book;
- is able to express opinions or feelings about main characters;
- is able to comment on reasons why the story was enjoyable.

Setting the writing test

In school the writing test will be undertaken by all children who are being assessed at the end of Key Stage 1. It may be developed from the stories the children have encountered in the comprehension and reading tests or from other work in the classroom. In this book, the writing test is developed from the work done on the comprehension and reading tests.

The writing test provides a broad assessment of your child's independent writing, covering his/her ability to communicate meaning to a reader, together with a developing awareness of punctuation and the conventions of spelling and handwriting.

What to do

1 The grids on pages 25 and 39 give suggestions as to the types of writing the children could do based on the comprehension and reading passages. From the grid, choose one idea as a focus for the writing, which may be a story or a piece of non-narrative writing.

2 Introduce the writing test to your child by:

- encouraging him/her to plan his/her writing;

- considering who the writing is for and the appropriate ways of organising it, e.g. letter, instructions, story;

- discussing themes, characters, ideas;

- exploring appropriate words and phrases;

- rereading the story;

- researching additional information.

3 This support must stop short of telling your child what to write.

4 You can give your child a general reminder about punctuation.

Test 1

Spelling picture 1

Spelling text 1

_____ I went to the _____ with my Dad.

We got lots of _____ things to _____ .

When we got _____ , Dad put the shopping on the _____ .

I had a _____ and he put _____ the shopping.

He made _____ and I _____ it all.

Comprehension test 1 – *Fiction*
William's Problems

William Barnes had problems.

Problem number one was that he couldn't get his 'b's and 'd's the right way round.

Problem number two was that his father had gone to work away from home, and William missed him. But that wasn't such a problem because he'd soon be coming back.

William and his mother talked about him a lot, and about how wonderful it would be when he came home.
It made them feel much happier.

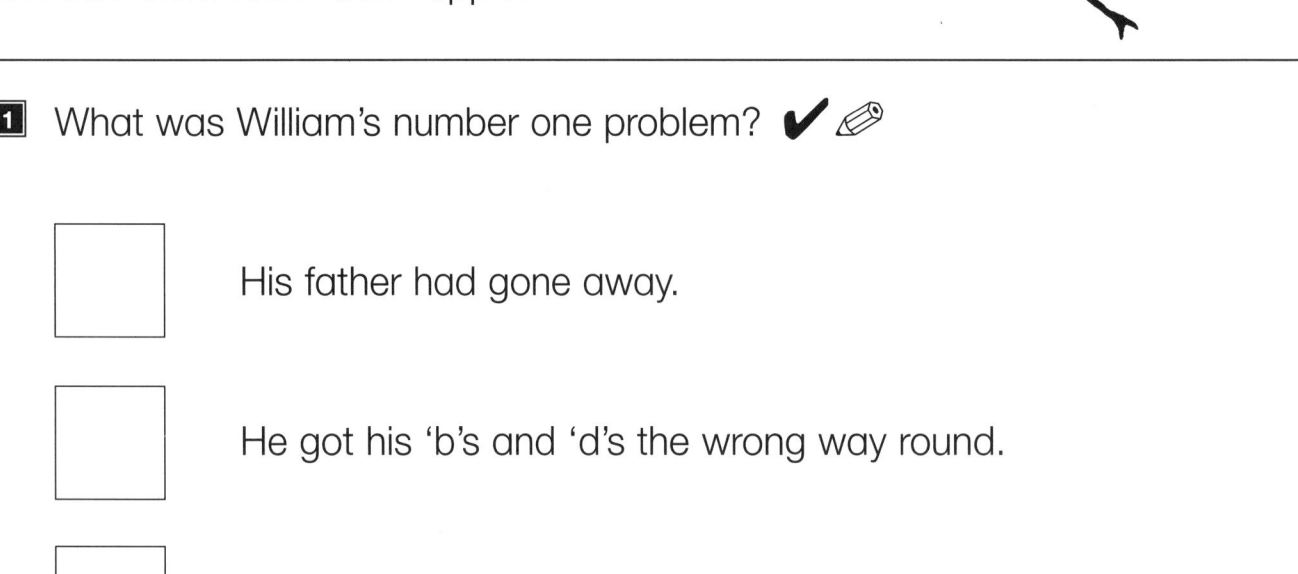

---

1 What was William's number one problem? ✓

☐ His father had gone away.

☐ He got his 'b's and 'd's the wrong way round.

☐ His father was coming back.

2 What did William and his mother talk about?

14

They told William's little brother Matthew about how wonderful it would be. But Matthew was only one year old, and didn't seem to care one way or another. He just smiled and waved his rattle. When you are only one you don't have many problems, thought William. William was seven.

---

3 How old was Matthew? ✔ ✏️

☐ seven   ☐ one

☐ three   ☐ five

4 What did Matthew do when William spoke to him about his father coming back?

✏️

_____

But problem number three was the biggest problem of all. William's grandfather was coming to live with them, and William would have to give up his nice big bedroom, so that Grandfather could move into it.

It was a wonderful room, and William loved it. It was big enough for him to be able to set out his model railway, and still have enough space to leave all his other toys lying about. William's habit of leaving his toys lying about was a problem, said his mother.

But William didn't think it was a problem – it was just handy.

---

5 Grandfather was going to sleep in ✔️✏️

☐ Matthew's room   ☐ the spare room

☐ William's room   ☐ the living room

6 What did William's mother think was a problem?

_____

The day came when Grandfather and his furniture would arrive. William and his mother sat in the kitchen.

It was the last time that they would have breakfast alone.

As he ate his breakfast, William thought about his grandfather. He hadn't met him very many times because Grandfather lived a long way off, right at the other end of the country.

But now he was coming to live in William's bedroom.

'Why?' asked William.
'He's lonely,' said William's mother.
'Is being lonely a problem?' said William.
'It can be,' said his mother.

---

7 What did William think about when he was eating his breakfast? ✔️✏️

☐ his room ☐ school

☐ Matthew ☐ Grandfather

8 What was Grandfather's problem?

William went to school. In the middle of the morning his teacher asked everyone to write a story about an animal.

William thought that he would write a story about a bad dog, who went round digging in gardens, and barking at everyone.

Then he remembered the 'b's and 'd's. If he got them the wrong way round it might not say 'bad dog', but 'dab bog' – which was silly.

So he wrote a story about a ginger cat instead. It was quite boring.

Then he went home and found a van standing outside the house. Grandfather's furniture had arrived.

---

9 What did William write a story about? ✔️ ✏️

☐ a garden ☐ a bad dog

☐ a 'dab bog' ☐ a ginger cat

10 What did William see when he got home? ✏️

_____

This is the beginning of William's story.

> Once upon a time there was a ginger cat. It had one eye because it had lost the other one in a fight. It was friends with a ~~a~~ black cat called Sooty. Ginger and Sooty were always together. Last week they went into the park.
> In the park there was a dog that barked and did'nt like cats. The ~~b~~dog jumped up and down when he saw the two cats.

11 How had Ginger lost his eye?

_____

12 Who was Ginger's friend?

_____

13 Where did Ginger and Sooty go last week?

_____

14 What did the dog in the park do?

_____

Comprehension test 1 – *Non-fiction*
Cats

Introduction

There are many different types of cat.

Small cats are often kept as pets or on farms to catch rats and mice.

There are many large cats. These live in the wild or can be seen in zoos or in game parks.

1 Cats are kept on farms to catch ✔️✏️

- [ ] insects
- [ ] rats and mice
- [ ] rabbits
- [ ] foxes

2 Where can you see wild cats? ✏️

_____

What are cats like?

Most cats have claws and sharp teeth which they use to hunt and kill smaller animals for food.

Cats will eat birds, small mammals and fish.

They can see very well even when it is dark and they have a good sense of smell and hearing.

When they are born they have no teeth and cannot see, but very soon they learn to look after themselves and find food.

3 What do cats use to hunt with?

_____

_____

4 What do cats look like when they are born?

_____

_____

Big cats

Lions are very big cats. They live in Africa and are known as 'kings of the jungle'. The male lion has a shaggy mane and lives with a group of female lions. These groups are called 'prides'. Lions live in grasslands and hunt at night.

Tigers are also very big cats. They live in India and have striped coats which help them to hide in the grass.

Cheetahs live in Africa and Asia and are also called hunting leopards. They can run up to 110 km per hour and are the fastest of all mammals.

---

5 Which big cats live in prides? ✔

☐ tigers   ☐ lions

☐ cheetahs   ☐ small cats

6 How quickly can cheetahs run?
_____

The Cheshire Cat

You can find the Cheshire Cat in the story of *Alice in Wonderland*. Alice falls down a rabbit hole into Wonderland. She has some very strange adventures. The Cheshire Cat has a very big grin, very big teeth and very long claws. He tells Alice where the March Hare and the Mad Hatter live and then just disappears!

7 Alice gets into Wonderland ✔︎

☐ through a door   ☐ on a magic carpet

☐ through a rabbit hole   ☐ by making a wish

8 What does the Cheshire Cat look like?

Reading test 1
William's Problems

William went to look at his old room. It was full of chests and a huge, old bed. The furniture almost filled the room.

'There will hardly be room for him to move about!' said William's mother.

'Why doesn't he get smaller furniture?' asked William.

'He's had these things a long time,' said William's mother. 'He's very fond of them. He doesn't want to give them up. It's a problem.'

William went to look at his new room. It was very small and tidy – for there was no room to leave his things lying about.

William liked to see his things lying about, and he understood how Grandfather felt about his old chests and his bed.

Writing questions grid

Idea	Example	William's Problems
Extending and adapting ideas or language patterns	A further episode of the story Characters used in a different setting Using a repeated phrase	William's first conversation with Grandfather
Informative writing	A data base entry or leaflet	A list of William's problems and how to solve them
Personal response/review	Comments to tell other children about the book or to recommend it	Writing to a direct question: Write about why you liked *William's Problems*
A personal account	Inspired by characters or events in the book	Having Grandmother or Grandfather to live with you
Alternative versions	Own versions of the story/alternative viewpoint	Tell the story from Mother's viewpoint
Letter writing	Questions or a letter to the author, illustrator or a particular character	Questions to Dad about working away from home
Instructions	Explaining how to do or make something	Rules for tidying your bedroom
Expressing opinions	Giving own viewpoint about behaviour or events	Would you feel the same or different if your Grandfather was coming to live with you?

Test 2

Spelling picture 2

Spelling text 2

Tom is _____ a _____ about a ship that is

_____ at sea. Each _____ the men look for

_____ . They have no _____ and very little food. They

must get home _____ .

Tom _____ the story and he _____ it will have

a _____ ending.

Comprehension test 2 – *Fiction*
Penguin's Progress

Otto was a penguin chick. He lived on his father's feet at the bottom of the world. That's what Leo said, anyway, that they lived at the bottom of the world. Leo was another penguin chick and he lived on *his* father's feet.

1 What were Otto and Leo? ✓

☐ chickens   ☐ penguins

☐ ducks   ☐ swans

2 Where did Otto and Leo live?

_____

_____

That is how Otto met him. Their fathers Claudius and Nero were friends and when they stopped to talk to each other, beak to beak, Otto and Leo were almost beak to beak too. They had to shout a bit because Claudius and Nero were rather fat, like all the other penguins, so their tummies kept Otto and Leo rather far apart.

3 Claudius was Nero's ✔✎

☐ friend   ☐ brother

☐ uncle   ☐ sister

4 Why did Otto and Leo have to shout? ✎

_____

_____

'How do you know we're at the bottom of the world?' Otto yelled across to Leo one morning.

'Your father told my father,' said Leo. 'Your father knows everything.'

'What?' yelled Otto.

'Your father knows everything,' Leo squealed back. 'Everyone goes to Claudius when they want to know anything.'

'I know that,' Otto complained bitterly. 'I can never get a word in!'

---

5 How did Leo know they lived at the bottom of the world?

_____

6 Who 'knows everything'? ✔ ✎

☐ Leo   ☐ Otto

☐ Nero   ☐ Claudius

'What are you two bellowing about down there?' said a deep voice above their heads.

'Oh, Dad, there are so many things I want to know about and you never even talk to me,' Otto shouted, looking up.

A beak came down and Otto looked into Claudius's face for the first time.

'I hadn't realised how grown up you are now, Otto. I'm not your father, by the way. Call me Claudius, not Dad.'

---

7 What does 'bellowing' mean? ✔ ✎

☐ laughing   ☐ playing

☐ shouting   ☐ singing

8 What did Claudius tell Otto? ✎

_____

_____

'Why aren't you my father?'
'Because I found you in the snow when you were an egg and decided to look after you and keep you warm until you could look after yourself.'

'Didn't my own father want me then?'
'Oh, it wasn't that at all. You probably rolled off his feet when he wasn't looking. Very rolly things, eggs are. Anyway, you're all right now. You've got me.'
Otto was worried. 'But I might have fallen off,' he said.
'Fallen off what?'
'The world. Leo said this is the bottom of the world.'

---

9 What are 'very rolly things'? ✔️✏️

☐ eggs ☐ feet

☐ penguins ☐ snow

10 What was Otto worried about?

_____

_____

'Well, it is. Antarctica it's called, the South Pole. But you won't fall off.'
'Why not?'
'Because I say so. What else do you want to ask me?'
'What am I?'
'A penguin. An emperor penguin.'
'I know that. I mean what is a penguin?'
'A bird. Now we'll have to stop talking and join the huddle of penguins, because the wind is getting up and it will be very cold soon.'

---

11 How did Otto lose his real father?
_____

12 What is the bottom of the world called?
_____

13 What else did Otto want to know?
_____

14 Why did the penguins have to huddle together?
_____

Comprehension test 2 – *Non-Fiction*
The Antarctic

Introduction

Antarctica is a huge land covered in ice and snow. In fact, most of the world's snow and ice can be found in Antarctica.

Below the ice and snow there are big mountains. In some places the biggest mountains poke through the ice and snow.

1 What is Antarctica covered in? ✓

☐ grass ☐ ice and snow

☐ trees and flowers ☐ sand

2 What would you find below the ice and snow?

_____

_____

What lives there?

There are lots of birds that live in Antarctica. You can find penguins, gulls and terns. They use the snow and ice to rest on and have their babies. They find their food in the sea.

You can also find many seals swimming in the cold sea, and many kinds of whales.

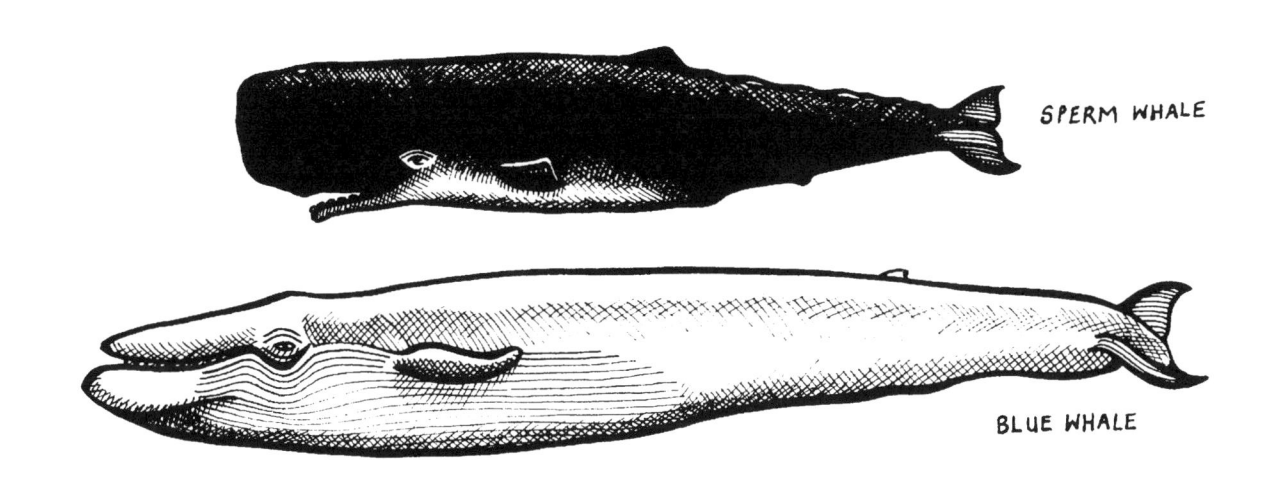

SPERM WHALE

BLUE WHALE

3 Write the names of two kinds of bird you could find in Antarctica.

_____

4 Which one of these is the name of a kind of whale? ✔

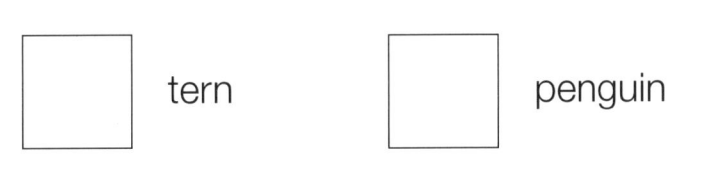

☐ tern   ☐ penguin

☐ gull   ☐ blue

Who saw Antarctica first?

The first people to see Antarctica were seal hunters in 1820, but nobody set foot on it until 1895.

Once it was known about, many people from different countries wanted to be the first to reach the South Pole.

Robert Scott and Roald Amundsen had a race to see who would reach the South Pole first. Scott got there on 17th January 1912, but he was beaten by Amundsen who had reached it in 1911.

---

5 Who was the first to see Antarctica? ✔️✏️

☐ Robert Scott ☐ Roald Amundsen

☐ seal hunters

6 Who was the first to reach the South Pole?

_____

Explorers

Look at the chart. It tells you about some of the people who have tried to reach the South Pole.

Name	Nationality	Date
Roald Amundsen	Norwegian	Reached the South Pole in 1911
Richard Byrd	American	Explored the Antarctic by air
Ernest Shackleton	British	Nearly reached the South Pole in 1908
Robert Scott	British	Reached the South Pole in 1912

7 Who reached the South Pole in 1911?

☐ Richard Byrd   ☐ Roald Amundsen

☐ Ernest Shackleton   ☐ Robert Scott

8 Who reached the South Pole in 1912?

☐ Richard Byrd   ☐ Roald Amundsen

☐ Ernest Shackleton   ☐ Robert Scott

Reading test 2
Penguin's Progress

'Soon!' squeaked Otto. 'It's cold all the time!'

'It will feel even colder if you don't join the other penguins. Come on.'

Claudius began to shuffle across the ice towards the other penguins who were already huddling together to keep warm.

'Aren't there a lot of us?' Otto yelled up to Claudius.

'That's good,' Claudius boomed back at the chick on his feet. 'The more there are, the warmer we'll be. Now keep your beak shut and snuggle as close as you can to me. There's a real blizzard coming.'

Otto did what he was told but it was very difficult to keep his beak shut. He wanted to know what a blizzard was.

Writing questions grid

Idea	Example	Penguin's Progress
Extending and adapting ideas or language patterns	A further episode of the story Characters used in a different setting Using a repeated phrase	What happens when the blizzard comes?
Informative writing	A data base entry or leaflet	A fact sheet about penguins
Personal response/review	Comments to tell other children about the book or to recommend it	Writing to a direct question: Write about why you liked *Penguin's Progress*
A personal account	Inspired by characters or events in the book	Being a penguin in the Antarctic
Alternative versions	Own versions of the story/ alternative viewpoint	Write what happens in the story
Letter writing	Questions or a letter to the author, illustrator or a particular character	A letter home from the Antarctic
Instructions	Explaining how to do or make something	Rules for going out in very cold weather
Expressing opinions	Giving own viewpoint about behaviour or events	Should people explore dangerous places?

Answers

Spelling picture 1

| plum | bag | sweet | milk |

| jam | cake | bread | butter |

Spelling text 1

Today I went to the **shop** with my Dad.

We got lots of **good** things to **eat**.

When we got **home**, Dad put the shopping on the **table**.

I had a **drink** and he put **away** the shopping.

He made **dinner** and I **ate** it all.

Comprehension test 1

William's problems

1	He got his 'b's and 'd's the wrong way round	1 mark
2	his father.	1 mark
3	one	1 mark
4	smiled **or** waved his rattle	1 mark
5	William's room	1 mark
6	William's habit of leaving his toys lying about.	1 mark
7	Grandfather	1 mark
8	He was lonely.	1 mark
9	a ginger cat	1 mark
10	a van **or** Grandfather's furniture	1 mark
11	in a fight	1 mark
12	Sooty	1 mark
13	into the park	1 mark
14	jumped up and down	1 mark

Cats

1	rats and mice	1 mark
2	in the wild **or** in game parks **or** in zoos	1 mark
3	claws **or** sharp teeth	1 mark
4	no teeth **or** cannot see	1 mark
5	lions	1 mark
6	110 km per hour	1 mark
7	through a rabbit hole	1 mark
8	very big grin **or** very big teeth **or** very long claws	1 mark

Conversion of score into National Curriculum levels

Marks	0–6	7–12	12–17	18–22
NC Level	Level 2 not achieved	Level 2C achieved	Level 2B achieved	Level 2A achieved

Reading Test 1 William's Problems

William went to look at his old room. It was full of chests and a huge, old bed. The furniture almost filled the room. 'There will hardly be room for him to move about!' said William's mother.

'Why doesn't he get smaller furniture?' asked William.

'He's had these things a long time,' said William's mother. 'He's very fond of them. He doesn't want to give them up. It's a problem.'

William went to look at his new room. It was very small and tidy – for there was no room to leave his things lying about. William liked to see his things lying about, and he understood how Grandfather felt about his old chests and his bed.

Level 1 questions

What part did you like best in the story and why?
Did you find anything sad in the story?
What sort of room do you sleep in?
Do you think it is all right for William to leave his toys lying about?
Do you keep your room tidy?
Where do you keep your toys?

Level 2 questions

Characters

Would you like to share a room with William? Why?
If you were William's mother/father how would you get him to keep his room tidy?
How do you think William felt when he saw the furniture van?

Important parts of the story

What were William's three problems?
Which do you think is the most important problem for William?
Which problem do you think will be solved first?

Questions inviting speculation

What would happen if …
    Grandfather decided not to come and live with them?
    Grandfather sold most of his big old furniture?
    William had moved into an even bigger room?

Spelling picture 2

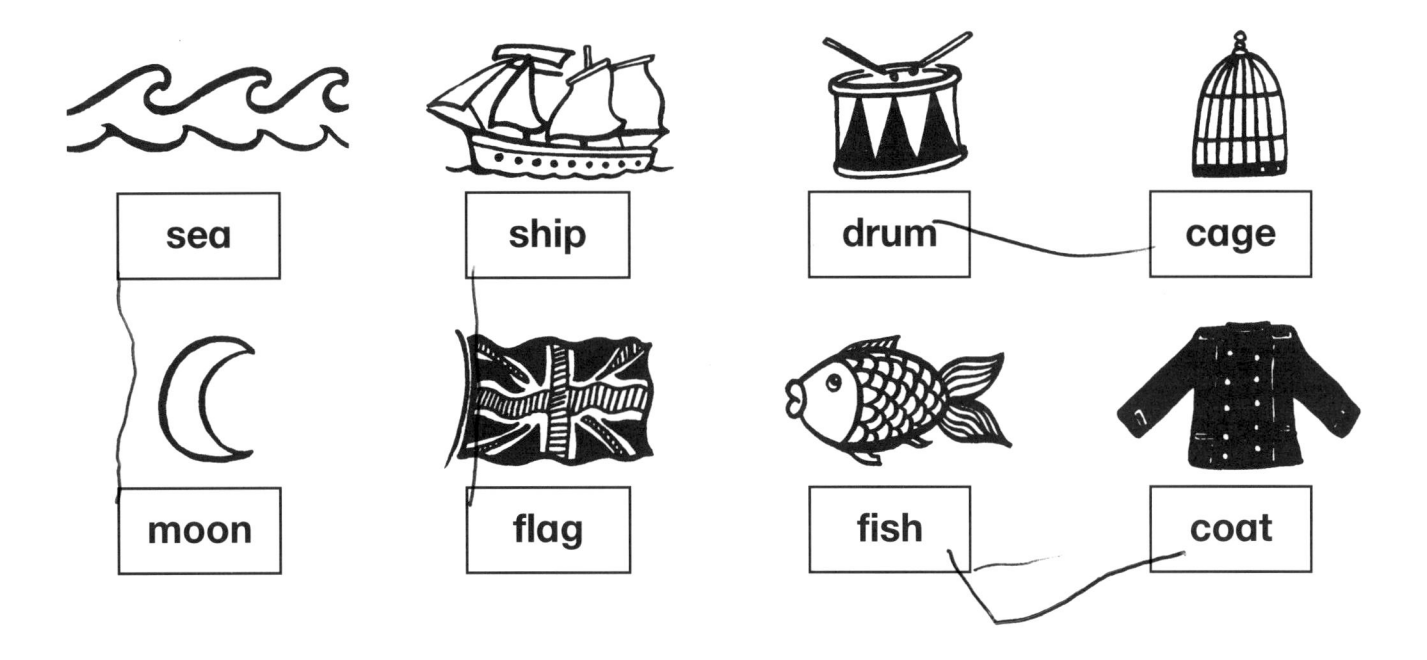

sea	ship	drum	cage
moon	flag	fish	coat

Spelling text 2

Tom is **reading** a **book** about a ship that is **lost**

at sea. Each **morning** the men look for **land**.

They have no **water** and very little food. They must get home **soon**.

Tom **likes** the story and he **hopes** it will have a **happy** ending.

Comprehension test 2

Penguin's Progress

1	penguins	*1 mark*
2	on their fathers' feet **or**	
	at the bottom of the world	*1 mark*
3	friend	*1 mark*
4	Their fathers' fat tummies	
	kept them far apart.	*1 mark*
5	Leo heard Otto's father telling his father.	*1 mark*
6	Claudius	*1 mark*
7	shouting	*1 mark*
8	that he was not his father	*1 mark*
9	eggs	*1 mark*
10	He might have fallen off the world.	*1 mark*
11	He probably rolled off his feet.	*1 mark*
12	Antarctica **or** the South Pole	*1 mark*
13	what he was	*1 mark*
14	because it was very cold **or**	
	to keep warm	*1 mark*

The Antarctic

1	ice and snow	*1 mark*
2	big mountains	*1 mark*
3	penguins/gulls/terns	
	($\frac{1}{2}$ mark for each of any two)	*1 mark*
4	blue	*1 mark*
5	seal hunters	*1 mark*
6	Amundsen	*1 mark*
7	Roald Amundsen	*1 mark*
8	Robert Scott	*1 mark*

Conversion of score into National Curriculum levels

Marks	0–6	7–12	12–17	18–22
NC Level	Level 2 not achieved	Level 2C achieved	Level 2B achieved	Level 2A achieved

Reading test 2 Penguin's Progress

'Soon!' squeaked Otto. 'It's cold all the time!'
'It will feel even colder if you don't join the other penguins. Come on.'
Claudius began to shuffle across the ice towards the other penguins who were already huddling together to keep warm.
'Aren't there a lot of us?' Otto yelled up to Claudius.
'That's good,' Claudius boomed back at the chick on his feet. 'The more there are, the warmer we'll be. Now keep your beak shut and snuggle as close as you can to me. There's a real blizzard coming.'

Otto did what he was told but it was very difficult to keep his beak shut. He wanted to know what a blizzard was.

Level 1 questions

What have you found out about where penguins live?
Who do you think was the cleverest penguin? Why?
What do you think will happen next?

Level 2 questions

Characters

How do you think Otto felt when he found out that Claudius was not his father?
What do you think Claudius and Nero talked about 'beak-to-beak'?
Claudius found the egg and looked after it. How would you describe Claudius?

Important parts of the story

What do you think is the most important thing Otto found out?
Otto thinks he might have fallen off the 'bottom of the world'. Could this have happened to him?

Questions inviting speculation

If you were Otto the penguin, what would you have wanted to find out?
If Claudius hadn't looked after the egg, what do you think would have happened?

Reading test assessment

[handwritten at top: how did Rhys be born]

Level 1

Reading with accuracy, fluency and understanding
In his/her reading of the story, your child recognised familiar words. He/she used knowledge of letters and sound–symbol relationships in order to read words and to establish meaning when reading aloud. In these activities, he/she sometimes required support.

Understanding and response
Supported by your questions, your child responded to the story by identifying aspects he/she liked or found interesting.

Level 2 Grade C

Reading with accuracy, fluency and understanding
Your child read more than 90 per cent of the passage independently and most of this reading was accurate. His/her use of strategies was sometimes inappropriate for the task, for example starting to sound out a familiar sight word. Your child read from word to word and paused to talk about the text or to confirm meaning.

Understanding and response
Your child commented on obvious characteristics, for example was able to recognise stereotyped good/bad characters. Any retelling of the story may have been rather short or too long and heavily reliant on looking at the passage.

Level 2 Grade B

Reading with accuracy, fluency and understanding
Your child's reading was almost entirely accurate and well paced in parts of the passage, taking some account of punctuation. He/she was able to read ahead. Your child sometimes noticed when the reading did not make sense, for example by self-correcting or making an attempt to resolve the problem, even if an unhelpful strategy was repeated.

Understanding and response
Your child commented on setting and on how the plot linked or contained surprises. Your child's retelling of the story referred to most of the main events and characters, although it relied more on having remembered the shared part of the reading than on the passage read alone.

Level 2 Grade A

Reading with accuracy, fluency and understanding
The reading of the passage was accurate and your child tackled unfamiliar words with encouragement only. Your child noticed when the reading did not make sense, and took appropriate action, for example self-corrected, looked back/forward in the text, or asked for meaning. The pace and fluency of your child's independent reading showed confidence, an ability to read ahead and the use of expression and intonation to enhance meaning.

Understanding and response
Your child was able to identify and comment on the main characters and how they related to one another. He/she was able to respond when questioned about extensions or alternatives to events and actions, and about feelings created by the story. Your child's retelling of the story was balanced and clear.

Writing test assessment

Performance descriptions for Levels 1 to 2A

Writing which you consider does not meet the requirements for Level 1 is nonetheless likely to show evidence of some attainment. For example, your child may use single letters or groups of letters to represent meaningful words or phrases, with some control over the size, shape and orientation of the writing, and be able to say what the writing means. The attainment of such children should be recorded as **W**.

Level 1
The writing communicates meaning through simple words and phrases. In his/her reading of the writing, or in the writing itself, your child begins to show awareness of how full stops are used. Letters are usually clearly shaped and correctly orientated.

Level 2C
The writing communicates meaning beyond a simple statement. It shows some characteristics of narrative or non-narrative writing but the form may not be sustained. Individual ideas are developed in short sections. The vocabulary is appropriate to the subject matter, with some words used effectively. Overall, the writing draws more on the characteristics of spoken language than on written language. There is some evidence of punctuation conventions being used to demarcate units of meaning. Some common words are spelt correctly and alternatives show a reliance on phonic strategies, with some recall of visual patterns. Handwriting is legible, despite inconsistencies in orientation, size and use of upper and lower case letters.

Level 2B
The writing communicates meaning, using a narrative or non-narrative form with some consistency. Sufficient detail is given to engage the reader, and variation is evident in both sentence structure and word choices, which are sometimes ambitious. The organisation reflects the purpose of the writing, with some sentences extended and linked through connectives other than 'and'. There is evidence of some sentence punctuation. In spelling, phonetically plausible attempts reflect growing knowledge of whole word structure, together with an awareness of visual patterns and recall of letter strings. Handwriting is clear, with ascenders and descenders distinguished, and generally upper and lower case letters are not mixed within the word.

Level 2A
The writing communicates meaning in a way which is lively and generally holds the reader's interest. Some characteristic features of a chosen form of narrative or non-narrative writing are beginning to be developed. Links between ideas or events are mainly clear and the use of some descriptive phrases adds detail or emphasis. Growing understanding of the use of punctuation is shown in the use of capital letters and full stops to mark correctly structured sentences. Spelling of many common monosyllabic words is accurate, with phonetically plausible attempts at longer, polysyllabic words. Handwriting shows accurate and consistent letter formation.